MUDDYING
THE HOLY WATERS

Chocolate Waters

Introduction by Nancy Slonim Aronie

Eggplant Press
New York, New York

Also by Chocolate Waters

Ladies and Gentlemen:
The Hudson Pier Poets, **Co-Ed.**

Chocolate Waters Live and Uncensored - CD

Charting New Waters

Take Me Like A Photograph

To the man reporter from the Denver Post

The woman who wouldn't shake hands

Acknowledgments

Many thanks to the editors of the following print and on-line publications where many of these poems first appeared: *Black Coffee Review, Shot Glass Journal, Big City Lit, The 2River View, The Pedestal Magazine, Sing Heavenly Muse!, Sinister Wisdom, Like Light, 25 Years of Poetry & Prose By Bright Hill Poets & Writers,* 2017 and *Brownstone Poets 2021 Anthology.*

I'd also like to thank my friends and sister poets who took the time to read this work in progress and offer feedback and suggestions: Jean Merritt, Red Washington, Jackie St. Joan, Heather Trobe, Marion Maxwell, Lynn Jericho, Rebecca Rikleen, Carol Bowden, Rob York, Peg Eves, Audrey Brunais, Mark Larsen, Hershey McClure and Elaine Johnson. Their listening was essential in shaping *Muddying the Holy Waters.*

Author photograph on front cover by Red Washburn
Cover & book design and layout by Lee Hannam @ yellowfishdesign

Inquiries and mail orders:

ChocPoet@Gmail.com
or
Eggplant Press
415 West 44 St.
Suite 7
New York, NY 10036-4440

You can also order online at Amazon.com (of course!)

What People Are Saying...

Chocolate Waters's new book, *Muddying the Holy Waters*, is poetry, but it's more than poetry; it's an autobiography in poems, an open and honest account of a person coming into her own through a tempestuous childhood. It's conversational and humorous, as in "Housefly Lover": Thot you'd be dead in a day / Google says two weeks / So here you are / humming and bustling around my head". It's funny and heartbreaking: "had I stayed / i'd have become a raging alcoholic / or a hallelujah / or just climbed into my coffin". It's edgy and rich with humanity and compassion, not just for herself, but for those she meets and knows. This book will captivate the reader, from start to finish.

~ **Bertha Rogers**, Poet: *Wild, Again; Heart Turned Back*

"Set this anguished world on fire" - what she tells us to do, and what she does herself, in her own poetry.

~ **Dr. Batya Weinbaum**, Poet, Writer, Ed. *FemSpec*

Live a raw and sensuous life. Suffer it with wisdom, wit and vodka. Then using elegance, restraint and bite, craft it all into hilarious, tender, brutal, outrageous poetry. That's the art of Chocolate.

~ **Lynn Jericho**, Writer, Counselor, Creator of Imagine Self

There are in this world a very few people who can make the language dance, so perfect, so accurate, so easy and so delightful, they can make you believe anyone can do it. Anyone can't. Chocolate can. Brava!

~ **Shelly Roberts**,
Columnist, Photographer and Author of *Roberts Rules of Lesbian Living*

"...sassy, irreverent, sexy, free-wheeling: sometimes scary and sometimes funny but always down-home honest."

~ **Colette Inez**, Poet, Guggenheim, Rockefeller and NEA fellow

"Chocolate Waters is brave, intrepid and funny."

~ **Robin Morgan**, Poet, Ed. *Sisterhood is Powerful*, former Ed. *Ms.*

"Behind a guise of humor, Chocolate Waters plants the seeds of discontent. She is a storyteller, serving up a feast of insights to the human condition – those things that, in the end, we know are the healthiest for us. A little Chocolate helps the medicine go down easy."

~ **Faith Vincinaza**, Poet, Publisher, Director Hanover Press

"Her work has a way of appearing light, easy to hear and entertaining, but all the while she's making complex, difficult connections and challenging statements."

~ **Jan Hardy**, Poet, Former Ed. *Motheroot*

"I really like Chocolate's poems, especially the one called 'Lyn Lifshin follows Me Everywhere.' It's lively and funny and original and full of surprises, like all her work."

~ **Lyn Lifshin**, THE most prolific poet ever!

"The sweetest Chocolate you'll ever know. She's terrific – read her – go see her!"

~ **Flo Kennedy**, lawyer, feminist, civil rights activist

On *The woman who wouldn't shake hands*: "This quirky collection of skinny looking poems, lacking punctuation, belittle the enormous territory they cover: it is nothing less than the human heart – that need for love and a corresponding need that guards against its fulfillment…No reader will be sorry to have read these poems…whose unexpected shifts, and word play share much with music. We hear what we read on the page, and what we hear will linger, like a melody, in our minds."

~ **Linda Lerner**,
Takes Guts & Years Sometimes and *Yes, the Ducks Were Real*

This collection would not be what it is without the discerning eye and wisdom of my dear friend, Lynn Jericho. She was always there with uncomfortable questions I didn't want to ask, insights I wouldn't have seen on my own. She encouraged me to "go deeper," to travel into spaces I'd rather not have gone. I am profoundly grateful for her support and for her friendship. She is a force in this world and the woman who has helped me become who I am, the poet I've become. Thank you, Lynn. Thank you.

Visit Lynn at www.ImagineSelf.com to check out her free blog post, counseling opportunities and course availabilities. Don't forget to sign up for her regular mailing list and her special Inner Christmas list. She will rock your world!

Contents

INTRODUCTION
Nancy Slonim Aronie

Chocolate Waters is a highly evolved human being. Her poetry sings off the page while her heart continues to pump its rich red blood into every line, every word, every thought she creates.

I've had the privilege to know Chocolate for decades and to witness her growth as a person and her evolution as a writer and spiritual being.

Muddying the Holy Waters, a collection of her journey from heartbreak to wise woman is personal but at the same time universal.

I have always taught in my writing workshops that we are alchemists. We can transform the mini murders of our lives into something beautiful, but before that transformation takes place we have to feel the sorrow of our story. Chocolate takes us there and we hurt with her and then celebrate with her.

Ms. Waters has done her work. Now all you have to do is read and enjoy!

Nancy Slonim Aronie ~ Author of *Writing from the Heart: Finding Your Inner Voice*. She runs the Chilmark Writing Workshop, teaches at Omega Institute, Kripalu Yoga Center, Esalen and the Open Center. She has been a commentator on National Public Radio and was awarded teacher of the year three years running when she taught for Robert Coles at Harvard University

IMPOSSIBLE

Dead in the Waters

You are so dead,
dead as those chunks of garbage
in the Pacific
that are twice the size of Texas.
You are so dead your deadness
is taking over the earth,
your planet not cared for,
your voice that won't let itself be heard.
Don't destroy the world with your absence.
Let your truthful voice speak, heal.
Let yourself love, whatever that means.
Set this anguished world on fire.

Gratitude
(for D.S.)

You dug up the dead poet I'd become
made me sparkle
alive with the joy of creation
You let me look at my relationship
to relationship
the hopes fears anger and longing
unseen weights brought to light
Thank you for the pain made productive
for the kindness of karma resolved
Thank you for releasing this
furious heart

Chocolate Waters, 2018

An Impossible Introduction

My life has been about rejection. Starting with mom Pauline and dad Emory who were excited about their first born until it was apparent I wasn't going to be like either of them. Not a little Pauline, or a little Emory either.

In grade school they called me "Choc-o-lotta Weirdo." At the time I thought the nickname was affectionate. The girls loved me and I had a lot of girlfriends, but the boys made fun of me, never wanted to be my friend, never wanted to go out with me. "Hey girl, your pimples are purple... Hey girl, your face is like an old Wingtip shoe...Hey girl, what planet are you from?"

I started writing poems. About rejection. Always centered on boys. If boys didn't like me, didn't want to be with me then what good was I? My high school years were a catalogue of rejections. Bill S., John H., Kenny W. – no one I liked ever liked me back.

In 1967 I had to find my own date to the senior prom. Randy. He was sweet and funny with dark almost-black combed-over hair that he was always pushing out of his face. Randy was from another school, a friend of my cousin, Carl. Prom night I drove 20 miles to Lancaster to pick him up. He was a fag, an early victim of AIDS, but I didn't know then he was gay. The thought never occurred to me. It was the early 60's after all. It wouldn't have made a difference. All I knew was that when the prom was over, so was our friendship.

I can't remember a single boy who was ever interested in me except fat, sweaty, pimply Lloyd S. who lived in a rundown trailer in Mount Joy with his alcoholic mom. He was the first boy I ever kissed, secretly, up in the old dilapidated barn behind the house where I lived then. All I remember is wondering whether that pimple on his lower lip was going to pop.

Later there was Bob from Marietta, another guy from the wrong side of the tracks. He had bad breath and no front teeth and later went to jail for murder. His saving grace was that he genuinely liked me, wanted to marry me. He was kind and looked like Elvis - for that I wanted to fuck him. When he refused because he "respected me" it was just another rejection.

So much for those early years. In college I discovered girls. OMG! Girls thought I was hot. A poet. A noncomformist. A smart smart-ass. I was cute, sexily brooding. My very first GF was neurotic, traumatized from being outed at a summer camp in Johnstown. She hated herself for her love of women – thought everybody else did too - but I was captivated by her intelligence. It was 1967. There was no women's movement, no lesbian or gay movement. Only bowel movement. I wrote her the first love poem I'd ever written to a woman, a poem with a man's name instead of hers. After about a month she decided it was just too queer to give each other those sexy back rubs late at night in the kitchen of the Russell Hall dorm in Lock Haven, PA. She dumped me out of her own self-hatred, but to me it was yet another rejection.

Nevertheless, I was discovering who I was and that there were people in the world who could love me. Women. As soon as I graduated from college I escaped with an old college BF. Bill W. Another closet fag, – but he had a car. I had great sex with him (still no fucking though – damn it). He was a jerk. His most exciting characteristic was making loud, wet slopping noises under his right arm and crowing.

We traveled the country for a while until I wanted to go to a women's bar outside of Denver. It was actually in Aurora; no one had ever heard of that place, until many years later when some wack-o gunned down a bunch of people in a movie theater there. Bill ended up taking off with a drag queen, left me sitting at the dyke bar alone, 28 cents in my pocket. Next day he left for parts unknown. I never saw him again, but I got picked up that night by Linda E., a towering, handsome, butch X-ray tech from Fitzsimmons Army Base. She took me in and saved my life. It was because of her I was able to stay in Colorado.

Soooooo, this brings me to the ten years I spent in Denver, 1971 – 1981. It was the beginning of the Second Wave and I was a part of that wonderful, exciting, turbulent time. I was a founder of the radical women's newspaper, *Big Mama Rag*, one of the first and best of the era. I met so many incredible, amazing, stupendous women – and I was determined to have sex with all of them. Rejection seemed a thing of the past - and it was.

Then I moved to Manhattan. I'd grown up in a military family and had traveled all over the continental U.S. Had gone to 13 schools by the time I was in sixth grade. I was nothing if not adaptable. Or so I thought. Trying to negotiate Manhattan, however, was like trying to negotiate South

America – I didn't understand the natives. I didn't speak the language.

Before venturing East, I had this fantasy that I'd meet up with Rita Mae Brown and she'd fall madly in love with "the wild outlaw woman from Denver;" my career as a poet would be secured and "all my trials, Lord, would soon be over." I was just peeping through my early 30's. The famous and connected women who had championed me in Denver disappeared. Robin Morgan had been a wonderful support when I wasn't in the neighborhood - even tried to get W.W. Norton to publish me. We had one lunch together and that was that. She liked me better as an outlaw cowgirl, not as yet another starving NY artist. Gloria Steinem, always gracious when I lived in Denver, was completely inaccessible. In NY I was just another…just another…just another.

I must add, however, that Jill Johnston made time for me, tried to get me connected to the Village Voice, really attempted to help me settle into the strange and inscrutable place that was Manhattan. She often called me just to see how I was doing. For that I will always love her, even more now than I did when she was my very first you-ain't-seen-nothing-yet-oh-so-outrageous lesbian icon of the late 60's and onward.

Later, Holly Hughes, who was then working her ass off to make the Women's One World Café in the East Village on 12th St. the success and refuge that it became because of her, took me under her wing. She kindly shared her apartment with me for the six months it took for me to get a toehold in Manhattan. I will always love and owe her a debt for that kindness. And OMG she was just so fucking funny and adorable!

Unfortunately, the small acceptances, the well-meaning gestures of support that I did get in those early NY days, barely lit the darkness of my lifetime of rejections. All the still births. All the miscarriages. All the impossibilities. Manhattan blew them up, magnified them in such a way that I just dropped out of sight - for 30 years. The world didn't want me; Manhattan's radical women's community didn't want me - so what else was new? Maybe I didn't want them either.

Soooooo - when the possible relationship with this woman who so intrigued me - the subject of this series of poems - came along, why would I think anything would be different? Why in the world would my friendship with her, my hope of loving her – why wouldn't it end up being nothing - nothing but impossible?

PREAMBLE

Encounter #1
(at the women's writing festival)

Room full of strangers
waiting for the poetry to begin
back row
She breezed by
Tall Honeyed Blonde Affable
"Are you having a good time?"
She glanced at me
not particularly giving a shit who I was
or wasn't
or if I was having a good time
or not
I wanted to say,
"I am now"
but my breath
stopped

Encounter #2
(writing on the wall)

J.P.s' workshop
One spot at the table
So excited I texted Red
"You'll never believe who I'm sitting next to!"
Five minutes later she'd re-arranged her position
moved backwards to
an open bench behind me
ten minutes later
further away
another table
this time way up at the front of the room
Workshop over
I slipped out
The hell w/her
No interest
Obviously
Then outside
Footsteps behind me
a voice
  "Hey Choc-o-lahhhhh - tee…"

Encounter #3
(more writing on the wall)

I knew she wasn't going to ask me so
I did,
"Can I take you to lunch sometime?"
Exchange of phone #'s   emails
We never talked again
but emailed
amicably
interestedly
I was away
visiting an old friend in a Michigan hospice
It was then I confessed my attraction
and got this response:
"I believe you had an intense weekend... So Sorry."
That's it? That's all? Dismissed.
I kept walking back and forth/one end of my apt. to
the other,
slapping my head w/the heel of my hand.
I'm so stupid. I shouldn't have
said anything.
And then...

IMPOSSIBLE
(from the first "ingest" to the last)

First Rush

longing to
ingest you
whole or
bit by bit
your stories
joys
sadness
wanting to know your
loneliness
your truths
lies
your journey to be more
first rush
of future embraces
pictures to be taken
in the Magic City or
Whiskey Hollow
or anywhere at all
wanting to write you
a first
perfect
rush

Possibly Impossible?
Or Impossibly Possible?

given our pasts
our loving relationships
that we killed
that we strung up
by the neck
& choked all the life out of
until they were so dead we
couldn't remember
they were ever alive
what would it mean to love
truly to love newly
perhaps we are impossible
the odds are not in our favor
& yet the possibility of loving you
makes me long for the discomfort
of the possibility of us together
of who we might impossibly be?

Fantasy

Sept. a.m.
sweet chill of fall
leaves mesmerizing
peeping thru the windows
big comfy bed
I snuggle into you
a little chilly
slip my body into yours
let you slip your body into mine
kiss you like I
never thought I'd
kiss again
Let me make you feel safe
and loved and safe and
loved
loved
loved

Her Response

I can't go there
I can't go there with you
You don't know me
I can't let you
Touch me
Feel me
Find me
Love me
I won't
Be
Seen
With you
I won't be
Seen
By you
I can't tell you
why

Apology

I left you behind
didn't I
so excited
to find you
I was more interested in finding me
I'm sorry
I should have
held you in my hands &
told you it's OK
Dear Heart
to feel something
anything
for yrslf or
for this odd stranger
who inserted herself
into your world
where you mean to stay
unaffected
where nothing
touches you and you
touch no one

Ice Cubes

2 trays full
1 cube at a time
2 at a time
a fistful
I hurl them against my front door
with all the force I can muster
FUCK YOU
for letting me think there was a
sliver of a chance
a soupçon of an
ice cube of a
chance
FUCK YOU for
being such a coward
I only wanted
to discover you
unearth our possibilities and
adore you
and you oh so politely
told me to go screw yrslf Dear Heart –
"thanks for trying tho…"

…all the neighbors
knew…

Tender Self Compassion

I'm sobbing
I'm sitting on the toilet sobbing
I'm trying
to wrap my arms around myself
on the god-damned toilet as I'm
sobbing
Shit
wrenching inconsolable human
Shit
I'm trying to wrap my arms around myself
and hug myself
like I did when I was kid and
there was no place else to be alone
There's no one else
who can hug me like I can
so awkward tho
dizzyingly uncomfortable
But OK ... let's try that –
OK...
Let's do that -
again

Dirty Karma

That's what Lynn says I incurred
sending you those first love poems
that I love
that I loved writing for
you
that I thank you for but
I sent them to say screw you
for not being able
to meet me where I longed to
meet you
for dismissing me
so perfunctorily
I'm sorry
forgive my inability
to see you
with compassion
forgive my
dirty ego
forgive
me

Things I Won't Have to Do
(since I'll never see you again)

Fix the floor w/duct tape
Paint over the mold around the sink
Paint the tub red (scratch that – install a shower)
Dust the dust
Grow another breast
Make the micro stop smelling
like burnt potatoes
Chase away the mice
Hide the denture cleanser
Toss the foot-high plaster bust of Elvis
Cure that pesky yeast infection
Throw away 100 vinyl records
Throw away 100 CD's
Throw away 100 books
Throw
everything
away

As Usual

Yr back to
bizness as usual,
taking care of yr flock, pastor?
You turned this
could-have-been-something-fabulous connection
into nothing,
into going back to watching tv.
Victoria is so much more engaging.
America's got more talent than us.
Go back to brushing yr
teeth in the morning,
at night tucking yrslf into bed.
No more sweet imaginations of
love, new love, almost love
to curl up with
No tender obligations.
No delicious dreams
of me   with you
of you   with anyone
Ever?
Just go back and
stay back.
You're back.
How good that feels.
How relieved you are.
Me too.

Bang Bang

She shot me down
as I was talking on the phone
She shot me down as I was washing the dishes
as I was watching Netflix
as I was peeing
She shot me down all day
all night in my sleep
She shot me down as I was walking the dog
(I made that up, I don't have a dog)
She shot me down thru sixteen versions of
"Bang Bang she shot me down, Bang Bang I hit the
ground
Bang Bang that awful sound, Bang Bang my baby
shot me down"
Thru a dozen new poems BANG BANG -
I shot her down right back.

Housefly Lover

Thot you'd be dead in a day
Google says two weeks
So here you are
humming and bustling around my head
trying to kiss the back of my neck, my lips
sallying back & forth across my naked leg
Stop that now
You know you'll die if I kiss you back and ingest you
There won't even be a body to bury
Good riddance
I'll miss you

IMPOSSIBLE / Chapter Two

HUH?!

Early morning ringtone:
"By the sea, by the sea, by the beautiful sea.
You and me, you and me, oh how happy we'll be…"
Sluggish cloud of sleep,
tune sounds familiar…
Grapple for the phone in the dark
white letters stark:
HER NAME
Head waggling back & forth shaking off the fog
I hear
"Thinking about your daring call…
You have a voice that could comfort the moon & the
stars…"
Truth is I'd drunk-dialed her weeks ago.
Tried to apologize to her recorded voice
for going faster than gangbusters,
for being too much – and too little,
for steamrolling right over her.
Tried to forget I'd reached out thru the drunken ether.
Tried to forget how she pushed me off the Empire
State.

"...tangled up in apartments and bed sheets"

OK, we won't go there
but please stop being more poetic than me
we can take it slow as snails
oozing along their glassy aquarium
slow as turtles fielding blueberries
slow as a long conversation over dinner
or a walk in Central Park
or a train ride along the Hudson
slow as my fingers tracing the back of yr neck
soooooooooooooooooo slow, darlin'
realllllllllllly slowwwwwwwwwww...
I can wait
to show you
how poetic
I can be

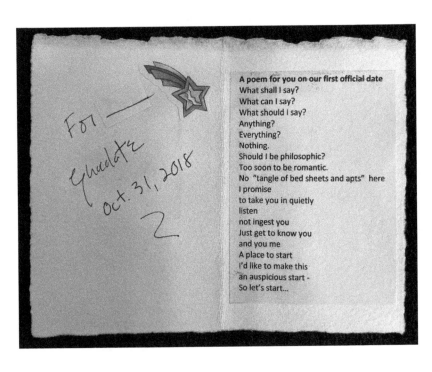

For ——

Ghadatz

Oct. 31, 2018

A poem for you on our first official date
What shall I say?
What can I say?
What should I say?
Anything?
Everything?
Nothing.
Should I be philosophic?
Too soon to be romantic.
No "tangle of bed sheets and apts" here
I promise
to take you in quietly
listen
not ingest you
Just get to know you
and you me
A place to start
I'd like to make this
an auspicious start -
So let's start...

32

Accused

"You are a vulgar person."
    What?
"That YouTube video where
you're acting drunk and crazy.
I think you were emceeing somewhere."
    Was I fat?
No answer.
    Was I young?
    What was the video about?
No answer.
    Was I wearing my Halston-sequined sweater and
    black leather pants with the sexy bowtie?
No answer.
    Are you sure it was me?
"Oh yeah, and
I can't have my name associated
w/such a boor."
    What The Fuck are you talking about?
Click.

https://www.youtube.com/watch?v=Qgz9aYaEiD8

"...stood up, broken-hearted again."
~ Ricky Nelson, Stood Up, 1957

I blabbered on
at my angel
told her I thought you might be the one
even after you threw a bus on top of me
squashed me flat   twice
I plead w/my angel for another chance
(tho angels don't care about such things)
This angel who sees all my lives
past ones   future ones
the one I'm filling now
My angel who doesn't guard me
but puts me in context
schools me in Truth, Beauty and Goodness
I thought I knew more
than her
more than Lynn, my brilliant friend
who knows me best and
loves me anyway -
I was wrong

You Don't Deserve Me

You know you don't
The nights I howled over your rejection
What tossing me out the window did
How little compassion you had
How oblivious to yr effect
You don't deserve the poems I wrote for you
Not the stunning ones -
I deserve to be writing again
I should thank you for that
But I don't want to
I wanted to write you more elegant poems
Not wrenching   angry   heartbroken ones
You don't deserve me but
I do

1 biggest fattest bottle of Tito's 6 packs of smokes 2 weeks Poems Poems Poems

I don't smoke
or I didn't
Not for a dozen years
I drink
not like this
not ever
I write poems
not these
not so many
Why now?
Why this?
Why you?

WILL THE REAL HALLOWE'EN MONSTER PLEASE STAND UP?

Oh, never mind, it's you
w/yr seductive Delilah mask off
yr Casper the Friendly Ghost mask off
yr Pollyanna Pure Heart mask off
But wait -
here it comes -
All rolled into one:
Frankenstein, Barnabus Collins and The Thing
Can't forget Dracula
Sorry Drac
No more veins to split.
No more blood to suck.

ANGER

I do anger so well
A+
Gold Star
Is it beautiful
how well I do
anger?
Wise?
Informed?
Awake?
Poetic?
Pavlovian?
Is it OK that I'm angry?
Bitter and snarky?
You did just
fuck me.
Again.
And you did that so well.

Curling Up

falling off to sleep
thinking of you
wrapping yr arms around me
my arms around you too
Now I've got all these poems
wrapping their words around me
not very pillowy
but so much softer
than the cacti and granite
you turned out to be
and they give me so much more
joy

DONE TURKEY

I am so done
like a turkey on Thanksgiving
This turkey is
done
being a turkey
You know they're so stupid
they drown themselves in the rain
the insistent rain
that beats
into their open beaks
as they reach
with gaping mouths
for the sky
Oh I never thought we'd reach the sky
it was some romantic fantasy
with some turkey
some other
turkey
some other turkey just like
me

AFTERTHOUGHTS

I Know I Said I Was Done

No drunk dialing tonight.
No more room for reconciliation,
re-connection.
No more room, so
why am I thinking about it?
I'm not.

*"Danger, Will Robinson, Danger!"
(relationship encounters of the worst kind)

You flail your robotic arms.
I flail mine.
Two aliens
each on our own planet
taking tiny mechanical steps
forward, then back.
Sputtering, spluttering,
pitching sideways –
nowhere to go,
each of us lost
in our own
terrified
space.

*"Lost in Space" was a TV series about a family that crash landed on an unknown planet. The show aired from 1965-1968. Robbie the Robot often warned his young charge, Will Robinson, of impending danger.

Her Agony

is not mine.
I'd like to understand it,
but I can't.
Is there sympathy?
Maybe.
Maybe not.
I can't travel in her skin,
her heart, her hurt -
much as I'd like to.
Her pain
is not mine.
Her experience,
not mine.
Her shoes are not mine.

Beyond Me

Her rejection
is beyond me
My explanations just projections -
It's beyond me
every time
we'd begin to get more intimate
she'd run away screaming.
I've said she has no empathy
or kindness.
I'm talking about myself.
A deer caught in my own head lights,
hypnotized by my victimhood,
a dupe of my own fantasies
and her seduction
I wanted to see her truly,
but I did not see myself.
She's beyond me,
just as I am.

Thank the Goddess I Won't Have to Take Off My Clothes Now

Enough said.

DEAD ANIMALS

Who Could Care about a Duck?

There was nothing more important to me as a child than my animal friends. My beautiful Lad, my protective Prince, my innocent banty who was never named. We didn't have cats because my mother didn't like them. Lucky cats.

Our pets met bad ends. Ends that were too soon; ends they didn't deserve. I can't remember a single one who died naturally. Maybe the ones who were sold or given away. They were blameless creatures but non-entities in the scheme of things. They either died of neglect or were just not important enough to be cared for properly or protected. They were just not seen.

My mother didn't see herself as an animal lover, but my father did. He should've been there for them, but he wasn't. The only pet my mother ever cared about was a French poodle she named Fifi; probably the only French name she knew.

There was no thought about what the deaths of my animal friends might mean to a little girl who cherished them. There was never any solace or consolation when they just weren't there anymore. What happened to them? Why did they have to die before their time? Why wasn't my dog there when I came home from school that day? Why did my family eat my sweet duck?

I fought not to be another discarded carcass, just another dead animal. Is it a leap to say my siblings turned into dead animals? They all stayed in Mount Joy, married and went to church and had kids as they were supposed to. How could they really be alive if there was no one there to love them for who they were, for who they dared to dream of being? How could they even know?

How could I?

DEAD ANIMAL #1: Lad

The first animal I loved
A Collie
Luxurious coat I grabbed with my
toddler's hands
buried my face in his fur
inhaled how delicious
he was
a little girl's best friend
One day I noticed this long pink thing
extending from underneath his belly
I cried so hard
I thought his insides were coming out
he was dying
I ran screaming to my dad
who chuckled but
didn't comfort me or explain -
Lad was asleep under the old Studebaker
when mom ran over him
No one ever told me
where he went

Me and Lad, Bainbridge, MD circa 1950.

Mom and Dad and Lad and me, Bainbridge, MD,
circa 1950

DEAD ANIMAL #2: Dead Duck

I don't remember if she had a name
or where she came from
or how bright her feathers were
I don't remember if she was a she
I remember how I loved her
in my five-year-old way
I remember that supper
and who ordered her death
I remember who cooked her
I remember who ate her

DEAD ANIMAL #3: Chickie

Another unfortunate fowl
a rescued chicken
I petted as I fed her back to life
One day she was gone
Sold
to a passing stranger
another dinner
for someone more important than me
Her name was Chickie

DEAD ANIMAL #4: Goldie

I don't know how she died
old age
hopefully
My very own parakeet
Sometimes she sat on my head -
When I held up my tiny forefinger
she alighted
She delighted
me
One day she didn't come
Dad said we needed
the money

DEAD ANIMAL #5: Prince

He was a Doberman Pinscher
allowed to lay on my bed at night
to protect me

handsome
regal
especially before they trimmed his ears
his tail
Those ugly white adhesive bandages
How I suffered with him

One day my brother, Bob, tied him to his bicycle -
when Prince tried to escape
the bicycle followed
I witnessed his terror

A few years later when I came home from school
No Prince
Mom was wearing a beaver coat that day
and Prince
probably thinking it was another animal
playfully nipped at the coat
Always terrified of him
Mom called Uncle Merle in distress
Prince had "turned" on her
Together they put him down

Prince , Grandma Waters'
house. Statesboro, GA.
circa 1959.

DEAD ANIMAL #6: Banty

Grandpa Buller was a pigeon fancier
Raised all kinds of unusual birds
This one had been abandoned
Left to die in the dirt
A bantam of unknown origin
So itsy-bitsy I tucked her in my blue jeans pocket
She nestled there
snuggled against me contentedly
her head peering out
She was comforted and comfortable and
I loved her so much that
I took her along
when we went to the Washington Monument
The amazed comments
The affection from admiring strangers
A few days later she went missing
Mom had given her away to a neighbor
who thought I'd been mistreating her
As soon as I found out
I ran to her door
A sobbing woman met me
Banty had died overnight
Away from my devotion
her precious trusting heart
broken

DEAD ANIMAL #7: Scruff-o the Wonder Cat

He was a stray I rescued from the streets of Denver
Wondrously big and furry he
looked like an ocelot
My friend, Katie O'Brien, quipped,
"Ocelotta cat!"
Of all the cats I've cherished
Scruff-o was my favorite
After I left Denver with a thousand bucks
and a suitcase full of clothes
he was always beside me
moving from place to place in Manhattan -
friends' apartments for a week or two
cat boarding house when friends were allergic
Hard to say who all this displacement was harder on
Desperate to keep him safe
I took him to Mount Joy
to be temporarily cared for by my parents
He was attacked by the family dog
Lily
A skinny white hyper German Shepherd -
Scruff-o languished three days in the basement
Never taken to the vet
He died there
Mom felt so guilty
she put Lily to sleep

TRANSFORMATION
(on the departure of Scruff-o the Wonder Cat)

My grief spills out upon the earth,
as endless as the journey of the Fool.
Of all the doubts that I have had
since leaping off the cliff that was my life.
Of all the deaths that I've been through
since landing in New York with just a suitcase
and my Scruff-o cat beside me -
No single one has broken my determination
to become my best of selves,
like Scruff-o's death has cracked my walking stick in
two.
Not the loss of all my lovers and my friends,
not the loss of the city that harbored me a decade,
or the loss of Humor, my muse,
or the sidewalk sales of my possessions,
or the theft of all my jewels.
So why should the death of this old scruffy cat
turn my eyes into mountains
and my heart into the thistle of a rose?
Because for seven years he loved me.
That's all.
And I loved him back.
And with his death he told me:
Sever your connections with the limitations of the
self.
Sever your connections with the past.
Then soar
             into the moment
                          like a fool.

Scruff-o, the Wonder Cat, Denver 1979

Fifi

was the only pet
Mom ever loved
A French Poodle
who lived a long and happy life and
died peacefully in her sleep
When my mother gets to heaven
it will not be Jesus she longs to see

Mom, Fifi and me, Mount Joy, PA, 1964

For All My Dead Animal Friends

Mountainous
Inconsolable
Unexpressed
Grief
blisters inside -
My desolation
explodes
I rage
My willingness to love
anything/anyone
squashed
Any aspiration to have children
annihilated
I peel off the layers of suffering
at the hands of those
Neglectful
Careless
Murderers
Pauline and Emory
my parents
I name you.

I'D RATHER BE A TOAD

(the Curse & the Blessing of Mount Joy, PA)

How Mount Joy Transformed Me
into a Pisser Poet

The people of Mount Joy barely exhibited any, but I didn't call it Mount Joyless until later – when I was far enough away to realize how desolate it was for me growing up there.

I'm calling this series "The Curse and the Blessing of Mount Joy." A curse, according to Webster, is "a prayer or invocation for harm or injury to come upon one." Mount Joy was a curse to me by its very existence. It did me harm by its neglect, by its unwillingness to acknowledge me or anyone who didn't fit into its conservative, small town uniformity. Mount Joy was a box of its own making and it liked it that way.

Looking back, even though I lived in a myriad of other states and went to 13 different schools before the family settled in "Joysville," I went through all my rites of passages in Mount Joy. It was a miniscule, nondescript, white, Nixon-loving Pennsylvania town, just less than half-an-hour's drive from Hershey. Hershey was the home of Milton Hershey, the religious racist chocolate magnate (he didn't let black people live there) who first made chocolate affordable for small-town America. Hershey smelled like chocolate; it even had street lamps in the shape of chocolate kisses. Living near Hershey was the first story I told about being called Chocolate. It seemed plausible – no one asked why everyone else who lived near Hershey wasn't called Chocolate too.

I hated everything I saw and didn't see in Mount Joy. My face was in a constant state of rage, perpetually breaking out in gigantic, miserable, boily pimples that I squeezed out at the mirror with a vengeance. I took it all out on myself. I was the child who wasn't loyal to my parents' lies. My parents' lies could've been told anywhere, so perhaps Mount Joy was an innocent bystander, yet there was nothing there to expose those lies. Nothing and no one, except me. I was constantly confronting my mother's deceit that she loved my father. I implored her to stand up for herself and divorce this man who abused her, this man who didn't love her. I didn't confront my father. I should have.

Nevertheless, I was emerging as the one who told the truth, but there was no one to listen. There was no one to support my observations, my distress, my audacity in reacting to the obvious. So I hated myself and I took it out on my face, scarring myself so badly that it took two dermabrasions to smooth down the vicious pock marks I created because I was expected to hold my truth in. For a long time I resented that I didn't get that third dermabrasion, the one that was supposed to have made my face as smooth as most other peoples. Now I cherish the remnants of my scars.

Living in Mount Joy was living in a tribe. I wish I could say it was like living in a tribe of wild Indians, only they were anything but. They were conformist and conforming. They were "Leave it to Beaver," Caucasian, Christian, Republican. They were cookie-cutter boring and there was no room for anyone who didn't fit into their prison, no room for anyone who kept them joylessly the same. There was no room for me.

I was surrounded by my mother's family, her parents, my grand-parents, aunts, uncles and cousins who subscribed to Mount Joy's lack of aliveness. This was my mother's tribe and the reason I grew up in Mount Joy. My father only consented to live there to placate his own anger and contempt for not really loving her. I grew up in the shadow of my father's guilt.

My father's tribe stayed in Georgia and South Carolina, the South, a place I never returned to as an adult because of him, because of my own southern racist redneck roots. My aunt and uncles and cousins on that side of the family were foreign to me, the patriarchal side of the family. I never wanted to visit them or know them.

I kept the Waters surname because of my native American connection, my own ancestral wild Indians. My great grandmother was half Creek and it was because of her that my father always said he wasn't white, he was red – though I never saw that this observation made any difference in his understanding of what it meant to be Black or any ethnicity other than white. It took me twenty years to get him to stop using the N word in my presence. I was sure he still used it when I wasn't around and this certainty was painful enough to make me have little respect for him and his lack of understanding. It made me want to love him less. I didn't though.

I kept the Waters surname because of its connection to being temp-estuous yet fluid, nourishing, powerful, rebellious, healing. Waters in all its manifestations was a wild Indian pisser of a name.

I'm presenting this series of poems as the woman who grew up near Hershey, the woman who transformed Mount Joy Marianne into something as delicious as Chocolate. But only semi-sweet, if you please. These poems are my way to understand what shaped me both as a woman and a poet. I'm presenting them to you, in all their rawness, anger, confusion – in all their early vanilla desiring to be delectable, so you may catch a glimmer of something to relate to in your own deliciousness. My biography may have different details than yours, but I know there is something in your own story that will resonate with mine.

So I offer these poems as a gesture of love, as a gesture of healing. If it hadn't been for the dark and bittersweet difficulties of my early years, I would not have matured into a beautiful and compassionate woman. I would not have become the "pisser poet" that I am today. I would not be sharing these stories with you and for you - and that is a blessing; that is the blessing of growing up in Mount Joy.

the curse of mount joy

i ran away
oh the freedom in escaping
the christian republican evangelists
i'd rather have been a toad
i pocketed my mistrust
carried it to colorado
turned into a stomping radical dyke
i'd have gone to india
and become a cow

i transformed my loathing
into hating the patriarchy
men all of them
especially emory my father
narcissistic dickhead
i let mom pauline off the hook
thought she was a victim
she was a
complicit cunt

once a year i return
at christmas
when jesus
is supposed to be there
their jesus
who lets them love me
even tho they don't have a clue
who i am

Complicit Cunt

OMG! I just called my mother a "complicit cunt." After countless years of thinking of her as only a victim, I've finally granted her the power of choice. The qualifying concept here is choice. She didn't have to be a victim. She chose to - either because of cultural norms and expectations of what a woman of her generation should be - or because she had no support for her own uniqueness - or because she just had no guts.

She went along to get along, as the cliché goes, and in doing so she was a silent partner in her own oppression and in her negligence of me, her abandonment of all her children. She was a complicit cunt, and I as the first born, was the one who got the brunt of her complicit cuntiness.

Granting her victim status has been my way of understanding, of trying to forgive her for not being the mother I longed for, not being the barest scintilla of what a mother could be. She couldn't see me. Could she see herself? She was unable to cultivate my intelligence or my difference. She couldn't see the poet in me. She couldn't see her own poetry in me.

I almost forgive her. I got to be a voice in the Second Wave because of her. I got to be my own voice because I felt she didn't have one. Yet while being lauded for my love of women, I didn't love my own mother.

I wish I could forgive her completely. I do have compassion for the way she herself was never loved or mothered, never seen at the bottom end of the queue of 14 other children. The part of me that yearns to know who I might have been had she been an ideal mother also knows that I'd never have been who I am without her. I'd never have become this outrageous, brazen radical version of me. This version of me wants to forgive. So thanks mom. Thanks for being the complicit cunt you were destined to be.

complicit cunts one and all

oh, don't be so shocked
haven't we all been one?
i was when i didn't stand up
for my mother when my father was calling her lard butt
or fucking other women
or publicly claiming she should be kept barefoot
and pregnant
and still i liked him better -
if i took her side would he value me as little
as he did her?

my mother was one when she didn't stand up
for me
or any of her children
or herself
she wrapped complicity around her
a soggy security blanket
warding off dad's demons and her own
safeguarding her life and her children
on the altar of compliance
an acceptable sacrifice?

how different our lives might've been
had she jumped up and down and shrieked,
called dad out for the monster he was
raised her voice to smash
the dung hill of abuse
she was always buried under

and you?
c'mon
you're here somewhere
you know you are
think about it.

pauline and emory
– pauline's story

when i asked how soon she knew
she'd made a mistake marrying him
she said, "Oh, about 2 wks. later"
she stayed
half-a-century
he was a poor georgia boy
from statesboro
so poor during the depression
he didn't know there was a depression
she was a poor pennsylvania girl
from florin
so poor she was grateful for
potato soup
or an orange at xmas
pauline was the next-to-last of 15 children
overlooked
only mothered
by her sisters
never loved
she thought emory was her first
and last chance
and emory…
he just thought she was hot

Mom Pauline in her 20's

71

emory and pauline
– emory's story

never got to ask when he knew
their marriage was a catastrophe
the hours spent over the phone
with uncle billy down in georgia
late at night
lamenting his cowardice
for not getting a divorce
he had another family
sandy and her kids
every fri. night
for 16 yrs. -
he assisted them financially
an abortion in there somewhere
my half-sibling who never wanted to be and
when emory died in the hospital
the only thing sandy knew
was that he'd stood her up
that night

i knew they didn't love each other

didn't take much to figure that out
and i
first and female child
crammed it down their throats
they suffered each other but
never in silence
bore three more
bob gary tena
the siblings i left behind
endured
pauline and emory's disgust for each other
i fled
they didn't

frauds

my parents didn't know
they were frauds
thought they were doing
what was right
the times
the culture of silence
their disdain for each other
glaring
no affection
only pretense
they cared about us
their four children
"in their own way"
what a crock of cliché
we all survived
didn't we?

mom, dad and the other woman

wake up mom
we have to get to the hospital
the doctors say he may not make it
through the night
my mother stirs
rolls back a sleepy eye
the covers shift
oh she says
that's too bad

when my father dies
uncle billy and i go to see
the other woman
secretly

she throws her arms around us
    wailing
oh dear god
    sobbing
how can I ever live
    shrieking
without him

at last
i sigh
the grieving widow

growing up story #1

when i was four we lived in beaufort, s.c.
just outside the parris island naval base
pauline made me wear dresses i hated
drab grey and white checkered things
always hanging off me like flour sacks
emory let me pick out corduroy jeans
soft   comfy   unconfined
pauline made me wear a little red hat
i was always swatting
the tassels that streamed down my face
and looked like the entrails of a chicken
i loved going to pre-school
could already read
was learning to write
from the brightly-colored plastic alphabet stencils
lorraine, the lady who rented the "little house"
behind ours
had bought especially for me
i loved going to see her
until one day her husband don
appeared in the living room
in his boxers
his dick hanging out
I ran out
told emory -
he exploded
my alphabet stencils
disappeared
so did don and lorraine

growing up story #2

the first time i knew i could read
i ran to pauline
so excited -
she was hanging wash
didn't hear me
wouldn't hear me
couldn't hear me
my favorite
black & white teddy bear
hanging on the line
soaking wet
limp and lifeless
misshapen
his black plastic eyes
careening in their translucent sockets
back & forth
back & forth
bulging out
right at
me

growing up story #3

scared to death
of you
dad
no idea what revolting thing
my toddler self had done but i
slipped a copy of the reader's digest
into my pants
so it wouldn't hurt as much as you
strapped me w/your belt

when 2-yr.-old brother bob
slammed his head against the floor
you bragged that you
"helped him down
so he'd never do that again"

I don't know why bob thought
he had to pound his head
into the hardwood floor
why you thought
he shouldn't
i knew the readers' digest
wouldn't always
save me

The Parental Units

I loved the Coneheads, Saturday Night Live's brilliant depiction of an alien family who came to earth and interacted with the 70's culture of the times. It was from one of those Conehead sketches that I latched on to the term "parental units." It was how the Coneheads referred to Earth parents.

From then on, I thought of my mom and dad that way. They were mysterious, robotic and as unknown to me as if they'd originated in another galaxy.

My mother, Pauline was the most alien. In my perception, even Earth wouldn't have recognized her. She was a distant heavenly body, but she was not heavenly. I spent my youngest years trying to reach her. I collected brightly colored bits of toilet paper and secreted them into her gravy bowl. I accumulated cute porcelain dogs and cats because I thought she might like them. I was too young to know she didn't even like animals.

Where was she when I was so excited to show her I could read? Where was she when I wanted her to help me save that dying baby bird? Where was she when the kids at school called me Chocolatta Weird-o? Where was she when I couldn't understand why the boys didn't like me? Where was she?

Emory, my dad, was a distant planet of another kind. At least he tried, sometimes. He was, however, more interested in being anywhere but where his family was. A Chief Petty Officer in the Navy, a lifer, he served his country valiantly, but did he serve us? He always wanted to be somewhere else, the Pacific, Korea, Brooklyn - anywhere his wife wasn't.

I think my dad would've preferred me to be his wife. He thought I was smarter and more complex. He once announced in front of my mother that I should be the one to balance the family budget. I was more interesting than her, more like him than any of his other children.

I basked in this admiration until I got old enough to hate him - for his misogyny - for his absence - for his inability to love. I remember him joking about how Pauline should be kept "barefoot and pregnant." Was it any surprise that in the 1970's I became what I now refer to as a stomping, radical bulldyke? OK. I was never quite that bull, but I was stomping and I am radical, just not quite in the same way I was back then.

I love those days though. I love getting to be the loudmouth, un-apologetic, angry man-hating dyke that I was in my 20's and 30's. I love all the women I loved then and still do: Jackie, Jean, Maureen, Linda, Peg, Mrf, Thana, Sergi, Thalia, Marilee, Darlene and Frances. I name you, women who, for the first time, made me feel worthy of love. I had a forum then (the women's newspaper, *Big Mama Rag*) to express my budding poet, and I love that the poet I was has matured and become wiser, softer, more compassionate, less angry. I am, however, still at heart that "pisser poet" my friend, Alan, says I am (yes, he's the one who gave me that wonderful epithet). At 70, I've reached a place in my life where I am starting to understand. I'm starting to understand for myself – and for you.

Pauline and Emory, circa 1950, Bainbridge, MD

pauline's daughter

it was impossible having you for a mom
no way you could've mothered wild-child
brilliant
pissed-off
melancholic me
i ran more circles around you
than a venn diagram
but what was it like for you
left alone to parent four young children

abandoned by your husband
who preferred the company
of any woman but you
i knew you couldn't love me
i was yet another female that
dad liked better
you pushed me down the stairs
when the lengths of your tolerance
for my smart mouth and
bad ass attitude
had been reached
i got in a few licks myself but i
still have that chipped tooth
only an external reminder

i'm always forgiving you for
the internal ones
the ones that have shredded
my ability to love anyone
the ones that have
razored away my love
for myself

Me at 17, outside Margo's house in Mount Joy.

mom pauline

93 in the nursing home
decorated   bejeweled -
the "lady who's always dressed up,"
hot tamale lipstick   soft blue eye shadow –
you want us to know you're still pretty
as you watch TV
win candy at bingo
match my sister at scrabble
go to church
you read books about billy graham, sarah palin, bill o'reilly –
no longer write poems or talk about your parentless childhood
or your cruel husband who humiliated you for being fat
or your first-born daughter
who grew up to be a lesbian

why are you still here, mom?
wouldn't you rather be watching tv in heaven with jesus?
are you waiting around for me to tell you the truth of your life?
it was you who hated men, not me -
you who was the dyke - not me

where were you when i needed a mom?
your own mom, repeatedly raped by your alcoholic dad,
no wonder you hated men, couldn't fathom me
your first-born daughter who was so much louder
than you ever had the courage to be.
i'm not afraid mom -
this daughter you never could talk to
this daughter who wanted you to talk to –
now here you are
hanging on to an unresolved life
and here i am
hanging on to a life

that may only be resolved if we
understand what we did to each other
and let it go
is it too late?
can we tell the truth
before you die?
before i do?

Mom Pauline at 93, Pleasant View. Manheim, PA, 2018

*Mommie Dearest
(After Joan Crawford, the nickname my mother gave herself)

Here you are
ringed with pearls
in your lace-lined casket.
Lovely lavender outfit
sister Tena gave you,
hair done just so.

The gold band and diamond wedding ring
you always wore,
symbolic of the covenant
that gave you
husband family financial security,
but not much joy.

Handcrafted wooden cross in your right hand,
on your left the copper bracelet
w/the religious icons from nephew Kyle.
He was with you at the end.
I wasn't.
He held your hand and soothed you,
told you how we all loved you,
how I loved you.

What do I say to your dead body?
This body that gave me life.
Your first most-difficult born.
Your most difficult.
I squeeze your hand,
thank you for giving me life
and for marrying the "wrong" man
so I could be born uniquely me-
a noble sacrifice,
though I doubt you ever thought that.

Here I am, Mom,
brushing against you
with my softest lips
kissing your sweet face,
sweeter than it was to me in life,
goodbye dearest mommie.

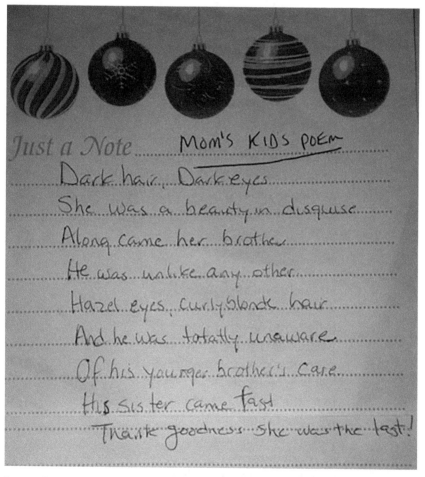

Just a Note MOM'S KIDS POEM

Dark hair, Dark eyes
She was a beauty in disguise
Along came her brother
He was unlike any other
Hazel eyes, curly blonde hair
And he was totally unaware
Of his younger brother's care
His sister came fast
Thank goodness she was the last!

I never knew my mom wrote poetry until I was an adult. This one about her kids, was inspired by an exercise I created for my Hamilton elders' poetry workshop. It was written just before she died and I'm pretty sure my sister wrote that last line.

emory's daughter series

#1

you were the man in my life
no boy could match you
i adored you
it was supposed to be that way
between dads and daughters

in a scowling pic of tiny me
sporting an embroidered jacket
brought back from your wartime sojourn in Japan
mom pauline had penned
"little emory"

just a facsimile?
i was a traitor by the time i could talk
making myself up as i went along
like you imagined you might?

#2

i thought you saw me
we talked about things
is there life on other planets?
where do we go when we die?
in another universe might we
just be a molecule
in a little boy's baseball bat?
we talked about politics
you were so republican
supported nixon
even when it was revealed
he was a crook
why did you say you were red
not white
why didn't we talk about that?

#3

when i came out as a lesbian
i couldn't tell you
we never spoke of it
we watched rush limbaugh instead
after you died i learned you'd read
all my dykey books
i never got to tell you how many lesbians
love their dads more than their moms
how we identified with the masculine
not the feminine
no matter what we said

i kept a dog-eared list of all the women i'd fucked
so many more than philandering you
i was proud of that
it made me more than equal
it made me formidable
it made me better
than you

My Dad was one eighth Creek Indian

waiting room

uncle billy and i were the hold-outs
everyone else had gotten bored with
waiting for you to die
mom wouldn't come
her anger made her unable to care
emanuel my evangelical brother-in-law
dropped by
last one to see you alive
he claimed three tears ran down your face
in the shape of a cross
he was sure that meant you repented
fat chance
i wasn't with you in your last moments
i was in the waiting room w/uncle billy
down on my knees in public
crying unabashedly
gasping so hard
my tears strangled me
praying to a god i didn't believe in
you were 70
why did you die so young, dad
why was i unable
to let you go?

Dad, 45, me 20, Pennsylvania woods, 1969

burning down the barn

m.k. and s. said i burned it down
the one in mount joy
where bachman's chocolate factory
used to be

first cousins
my heroes
i was 8
they were
five years older
"Flicking your cigarettes like a big person"
camels i stole from uncle carl
stubby unfiltered
we smoked ecstatically
chewed dentyne
on the way home
drenched our hands in loud perfume

fifteen minutes later
explosion
barn overwhelmed by sudden flames
three-alarm fire
or was it four?

earsplitting trucks
miles of hoses
parapets of water
people rushing breathlessly
"Run lady run!"
whooped m.
the smart-ass
not realizing the woman was running
to our burning barn

the three of us stood silent
on the sidelines
innocent as the gum in our pockets
until m.'s boyfriend, d. showed up,
"You did it, didn't you?"

the cousins sat me down
stern warnings
adult admonitions
"You were never there.
none of us was there.
they'll send us to a home."

that night i lied
to my mom
aunt maude
anyone who'd listen
where i'd been
who i was with
what we were doing
though no one
even asked

sixty years later
the names are disguised
except my own
and uncle carl's and aunt maude's
who are dead and don't care -

those three impudent kids
the blazing barn
smoke
conflagration
"Run lady run!"

that home
still waiting
for me.

Who Flicked the Ashes?

M.K. and Sandy assumed it was me. I was the youngest of the cousins, the one it was easiest to blame, just because the five years between us made me the most easily culpable. I was the suspicious baby, but they were babies too. Thirteen-year old babies.

We burned down that old, mysterious dilapidated barn, the one near Bachman's Chocolate Factory in Mount Joy. M.K. says she always thought it was an old house. How different is each of our recollection? A barn? A house? A milestone in my own life. What was it for my teen-age cousins?

Nevertheless, we set that old building ablaze, gave it a life it had not experienced during its long history of life and decay. We transformed it into a conflagration that made everyone come and see. We made that old barn matter and we did it together. Am I the one who actually flicked the ashes from Uncle Carl's pilfered cigarettes? We'll never know. We were three complicit cousins and we were having a hell of a good time.

Of course, we couldn't tell anyone of our accomplishment. We lied about being anywhere near the vicinity. Sandy's Mom, Aunt Pearl to M.K. and me, lived right down the road on Square Street. The three of us were in her living room when we heard the fire engines being called out. To us it seemed like there were hundreds of them. There were probably four or five. Maybe three… - two?

We stood on the sidelines, terrified. Me and M.K. and Sandy. We were peeing ourselves. Had we done this? What did it mean? Would we be discovered? Would we be sent into juvenile detention?

Later that night, I was having dinner with Aunt Maude and Uncle Clyde. I was petrified. I was guilty. I knew I was going to be sent to a home. Aunt Maudie talked about the fire that day. How did it happen? Who could've done it? "

"Probably some kids smoking," I offered.

Oh my God! Why did I say that?! What the hell is wrong with me? I am so stupid!

To this day I don't know why I blurted that out, but I suspect it had something to do with the fact that I was changing, both physically and in the way I wanted to be perceived by the world. I was no longer the small-town, accepting child who existed as the person everyone wanted me to be, the person I was expected to be. I was myself. I was unique. I was a bad ass and I wanted to be recognized for that. Was the fire just an accident? I probably am the one who flicked those ashes. It was my first step in becoming me.

Me , 7 and Marion Kay, 12 - Beaufort, S.C. 1956

APRIL 24,1958

Dear (I guess you know your name by now).

I'm sorry I didn't write sooner but I was just too busy.

Boy is it ever warm down here!!!! I mean its not warm its
just plain hot. This will be a fine time to go to the pool.

All I'm making in school is A and Aplus and such good
marks. I'm sick of making such marks. Why doesn't that teacher
of mine brake down and give me a bad mark? I wish she would.
What kind of marks do you make in school?

DID I ever tell you that we   went to see the
"Blue Angles"? Boy they did all kinds of tricks in the air
and they also let out colored. That was really pretty.

They would also make diamond formation. When you would think there
was only 4 plains here would come 1 Or 2 plains sneaking
up on you. And the noise they made was enough to scare you
half out of your wits. They would come really close too.

Yesterday a man came over to help daddy cement
in the patio. They had some cement left over so they put it
out in the back yard and made ort of a walk. The next day daddy
said that the cement was to thin". So we had to get the ax
and the shovel and get all of that cement out of there
and throw it over the fence. Boy was that ever a job.

Well I guess I'd better say good by
for now. So Ill see you in your next letter
that is if you dont get mad and dont feel
like writing.

LOVE

MARIANNE

P. S. PLEASE WRITE SOON!!!!!!!

First love letter 😊
97

marion "the barbarian"

you were my first love -
i was pre-pubescent
you were a teenager
never a chasm to us

as i grew up
you were my person
the one whose sense of humor
was weirder than mine
my anchor
in a small-town sea of sameness

to you i confessed
my aloneness
desolation
my painful guilt around self-love
you warned that touching myself like that
might make me queer
you were right 😊
when i came out years later
i assured you there was no physical attraction
didn't want to scare you
but you retorted,
"Well, why not?!"
others had their own ideas
like brother bob,
"I didn't know marion was bisexual."
i never told you there was a time
i had such sizzling dreams
they set the bedsheets on fire
(and i'm not admitting it now)

you were always my hero, my idol
this karmic connection
has sustained us a lifetime
you now 75
me 70 and
if we live
to reach 100
you'll be my last love too.

At Marion's place. Mount Joy, 2017

wish you'd have been my big brother, bob

you were a germ of a person
when you confessed your sins
at the altar of the baptist church in jacksonville
i was two years older and outraged
what the hell did you have to confess?
knew then i'd never be a christian
we called you butterball
chubby cheeks   blonde curls
when we moved to virginia
i protected you from neighborhood bullies but
i beat the crap out of you instead
one day
you grew up
punched me back
became an oak tree
kept the same job
forever
chemical engineer at armstrong
married your high school sweetheart
thought you'd stay with her
forever but
she left and
you hoarded cats
17 at last count
the ones who love you
these cats
and jesus
every sunday you're
a devout evangelical liturgist
booming sonorous voice
beloved by the congregation

you are as terrified
of me
pagan dyke poet telling my truth in a bar
as i am
of you
good christian
telling yours in a church

Bob at Glossbrenner, Mount Joy, PA 2018

Me and, Bob, San Diego, CA. 1953.

to my beloved little brother, gary

barely five when you
kicked that porcelain fixture
into the next world
that fixture would never hold toilet paper
again
you were a force
furiously devilish
with a loving
irrepressible
sweetness
i watched when dad almost broke you
he thought he was helping -
those menacing flash cards
supposed to make you read properly
my 12-year-old self powerless
as dad huffed and puffed and
blew our tiny trailer into a ditch
blew us all
into a ditch
those god damned flash cards
he thought he could beat you into learning
you'd flunked first grade hadn't you
no son of his could be stupid
you were just
dyslexic

gary, you're a wizard
of clocks
computers
cabinet-making
the smartest and most artistic
of us all
you astound me
yet here you are in your 60's

marriage in the can
daughter you wish had been a son
to share your genius with
asking me
if you could have done something different
with your life

Our trailer. I'm there at the top, look close. Mount Joy, PA. 1960's.

you murdered me

destroyed what i cherished
ripped my books to shreds
stole my mercury head dimes
magic-markered my precious pillows
i'd created in brownies
it looked like i was the one dad loved
straight a kid
spelling bee champ
the one who could read
i didn't know any of that
i wish i had
and now
can i'm sorry
make up
for anything?

Gary at Christmas, Mount Joy, 2017

devil siblings

that was us.
we didn't fit in.
you were high-spirited, rowdy,
too smart for what they were selling.
  "Well, if there's no santa claus
   there's no jesus either."
you were more logical than me.
we could've been allies.

Me and Gary, Beaufort, SC. Early 50's.

What Good Are Brothers?

Bob, two years younger, was my closest sibling. I considered him my friend, not an adversary. Not a sibling I had to be wary of, like Gary. Bob was an affable soul, slow and deliberate, often disheveled. His dishwater-blond curly hair ran amok and he wore suspenders that were always a bit lopsided. Nevertheless, he was genuinely sweet, never threatening and he looked up to me, his big sister. I didn't look down on him. I liked him, but I didn't think about him much. He was just there, another sibling, second in line. Had anyone tried to hurt him though, they had me to contend with.

Gary, four years my junior, was another matter. Wiry and ambidextrous with mischievous impish eyes that flashed like sparklers when he was angry. He didn't give a shit. Not about me. Not about anyone. At the time I didn't see this as a positive trait. Looking back, I understand this was his way of surviving the absurdity that was our family. He was unique, independent, and unapologetic for who he was. He got no support for that.

Bob had a lot of love inside. It was innate. If you needed something, Bob would try to provide it. That's the way he was. He never questioned anything. He just accepted things as they were and it was all OK with him.

Gary, on the other hand, didn't buy it. He didn't buy anything. If he wanted to help you he would. On his own terms. If he didn't, you could go fuck yourself. Gary had a lot of love inside him too. He just didn't express it in the way anyone thought he should.

As the big sister I was mostly absent. My teenage years were so impossible I could barely think about anyone but myself. At 14, I was tall, nearly 5'8" and stringy. I weighed 110 pounds and had such merciless acne that I knew I was the ugliest person alive. I didn't know what my role as a sister should be. I couldn't even consider it. My younger siblings were my blood and I was supposed to love them. In my own way, I did. But "in my own way" covers a multitude of sins.

What good were these brothers? They were younger so the question of them protecting me didn't really apply. I was the one who sometimes got to be the protector. I was able to stand up for Bob when he was in the sites of bigger, menacing boys. One of them, a 16-year-old thug with a big mouth and the belligerent attitude of someone who'd probably been abused himself, came after me with a five-foot wooden stick. I stood up to him, told him to stay the hell away. I was less than half his age – and size – but I was so angry that I somehow managed to wrestle that stick away – and club him with it. This earned me such a bad-ass reputation that other neighborhood boys would randomly show up at the front door asking if Bob's sister could "come out and fight today." I'm not sure who they were asking for permission.

I wanted to protect Gary too, but I couldn't. In his well-intentioned efforts to ensure that Gary could read, Dad was abusing him. My little brother was being battered by good intentions. I wanted to scream at Dad to stop, to leave Gary alone. To just back off and go fight in a war or something. I wanted to beat Dad with a five-foot stick, but he was way older than my former 16-year-old adversary - and I knew he could be way meaner.

Bob is the one who bolstered my confidence, my trust that I could stand up against a bully, against anybody. I have him to thank for not being afraid to face down people and situations larger and more powerful. He revealed my ferocity, a trait I've been able to count on throughout my life. He allowed that core part of me to blossom and to become the tempestuous child it is.

Gary. I thought he hated me and I, sure as shit, couldn't stand him. He was a vile, insufferable Roman-soldier-wielding sword in my side, always assaulting me with his fury and mistrust. I got to be the brunt of his incomprehensible wounds and I took it personally. I didn't understand his vulnerability, his tender hurt. Gary's lessons took me a long time to learn. I'm still learning them, but he's made me look beneath the surface of people's hatred and fear. Homophobes. Misogynists, Racists. Xenophobes. Trump supporters. It probably has very little to do with me.

So what good are brothers? More than I thought, more than I have the ability to say.

sister tena

the photo shows you crawling across the floor
bringing gary's shoe to him
that old black and white kodak print
pinking-sheared at the edges
your expression entreating
looking for approval
you've spent your life
looking for approval
i've spent mine looking for
disapproval
we are both slaves
i ran away to denver
at 19 you followed
sniffing at freedom
you disregarded it
returned to mount joy
to be the dutiful daughter of emory & pauline
but you never rejected me
and i never rejected you

Chocolate and Tena. Grandview Elementary, circa 1960.

why do you read my poems, tena?

i'm not saying anything you want to hear
i'm the queen of betrayal
never deferential
or loyal
to our family
a husband
god and the church
you're the queen of obedience
never questioning -
the queen of who they wanted you to be
i'm the queen of who they never expected
i've suppressed my ability to love
you've suppressed your ability to rage
i don't care if you never read another poem
you're the best sister
the sister who has my back
the sister i count on
the sister i love

Choc and Tena, 2006

111

What a Wedding!

Tena and Emanuel celebrated their 40th wedding anniversary in June, 2019. It took me nearly that long to apologize for the short story I wrote satirizing her wedding. Satirizing is, of course, a nice way of saying poking the hell out of. The story, "I Was A Christian Bridesmaid" was pretty damn funny. It still is, but what it cost in hurting my sister is not. I was barely 30 when I agreed to be my sister's Maid of Honor. It was a time in my life when I questioned everything I'd been brought up to believe. A supreme all-powerful God who expected me to follow his rules. A supreme all-powerful family who expected me to follow theirs. At the time, I thumbed my nose at both, but I loved my sister so I agreed to put on the beautiful dress she had made for me and for the other more-willing bridesmaids. I was trying to fit in with her expectations of what a big sister should be. I was trying to adhere to some semblance of loyalty to my familial tribe and I was truly happy for her that day, despite my reservations.

The wedding in the Hershey Rose Gardens in PA, was special, spectacular and I think, everything my sister hoped it would be. To make light of this occasion might have caused any other sister to hate me forever. She had every right to. She didn't.

At the time, I'd just escaped from small town, smothering Mount Joy, PA and moved to the promising land of pioneering Denver, CO. I'd chopped off my shoulder-length hair, an initial gesture of saying fuck you to any traditional idea of being a woman. That was only the first step. I became involved with a progressively radical group of women who wanted not only to change the world, but to blow it the hell up. We were exploring our own identities, both personally and politically and sexually. We longed for the gesture of the feminine, the embodiment of what it would be like if the values of the feminine ran the world. We thought this meant destroying masculine ideology. The Patriarchy. The system we lived in that had no respect for life, for love, for beauty, for real freedom. We wanted to obliterate that world as we knew it in the 1970's. We were naïve, idealistic, but we had the best intentions.

Yet what I did in savaging my sister's wedding was not loving, not compassionate, not funny, not Sophianic in the way we wanted the feminine principle to influence a patriarchal world.

My sister has endured me in spite of questioning everything she believes in, as I have endured her in spite of everything I believe in. This is beauty, compassion, freedom. This is love. This is the true feminine principle. My sister embodies this in her love and acceptance of me, as I hope I embody it in my love and acceptance of her.

Tena, the bride, and Choc, the maid of honor.
Hershey Rose Gardens,
Hershey, PA. June 2, 1979.

Me and Tena outside the RV trailer where we
went to make sure we were looking perfect.

My long-time friend, Jean Merritt (left) and cousin,
Margo Fry (middle) and me.

i apologize to you, my sister

for demolishing your wedding
in words and then publishing it,
humiliating you and your beliefs
in front of the world,
tarnishing your happiness.
i was young
pissed off
self-righteous
cruel.
that afternoon
at the linden diner in lancaster
i said i was sorry -
nearly four decades later -
i'd missed my train.
we had time.
it's a different time.
you forgave me long ago.
if i forgive myself
will that be OK?
is it time?

big sister (for bob, gary & tena)

never gave a shit about you
your songs of yourself
i left you
road kill
why should i have protected you
no one protected me
why should i have loved you
did anyone love me?
does that make a difference?

big sister 2

how did i fail you
*"let me count the ways"
i couldn't protect gary
from the wrath of our father
couldn't shield bob
from his own innocence
i couldn't warn tena
about mom pauline
i couldn't
could i?

*"How do I love thee? Let me count the ways." Elizabeth Barrett Browning, Sonnets of the Portuguese.

big sister 3

what did you expect from me?
should i have stayed
swallowed the lies
that choked you into the
complacent lives you lead?
should i have hidden
under a basket of jesus loves you?
a basket of mom & dad love each other?
a basket of going to hell
in a hand basket?
i questioned everything
you believe in
still do
and yet
who would i have become
what would my life have meant
w/out you?

At the National Spelling Bee in Washington, D.C. 1963

SPELLING BEE

That awful photograph.
14, worst case of acne
in the United States.
My very best dress,
midnight-blue organdy
poofing out at the bottom like a bell;
Matching blue glasses – speckled blue,
they looked like a
Chrysler hood ornament.
"These are the faces of a champion,"
proclaimed the words underneath
as Miss _____ Waters
 - aha - you thought I was going to
tell you what mom named me didn't you? –
takes home the 1963
Lancaster County, Pennsylvania
Spelling Bee Championship."

Another photo in the paper that morning -
me and my three younger siblings:
Vanilla, Butterscotch and Strawberry.
OK - Bobby, Gary and Tena.
Munchkins then, no taller than tree stumps,
so proud of their big sister -
they liked her in that moment,
they really really liked her.
Pauline and Emory beaming,
as proud parents will.
And the accolades!
Boisterous applause!
Standing ovation!
The look of unmitigated astonishment
on my first cousin's face -
Marion Kay - my cool cousin,

now grown up to be muscle-bound Marion
the Barbarian weightlifter.

And the prizes!
A transistor radio!
A heart-shaped plaque
(which I thought could've
been a little bigger).
A complete 23-volume set
of the Encyclopedia Britannica!
Dad promised 50 cents for every 1,200-page
itsy-bitsy-teensy-weensy-printed volume that I read.
WOW!
And the promise of a steak dinner from my favorite
teacher,
Mrs. Jessie Malmborg. Never delivered.
When you read this Mrs. Malmborg –
"I want that steak dinner!"

But most excellent of all -
an all-expense-paid-week-long vacation
to the Capitol of the World, Washington, D.C.!
BY MYSELF!
Well no,
with the reporter from the Intel, Larry Bauman and…
mom.

So, the big bee in D.C. came.
My spelling bee teacher came.
The high school principal came.
Mrs. Malmborg did not come.
I flunked out in the third round.
The Intel reporter reported that I cried,
which I did not.
At least not then.
Later in my room at the Mayflower Hotel

I sobbed into the bathroom mirror,
gasping out every word of "Climb Every Mountain,"
Even getting Harry Truman's autograph in the lobby
of the Mayflower Hotel the day before
could not assuage my utter misery.
I was a failure, a flop, an enormous disenchantment.
How could I ever grow up to be President now?
I didn't even know that girls did NOT
grow up to be President – then.

Only word in the entire round of 67 words
I could not spell:
 "ferret" –
the pronouncer said it was "furry."
It's not "furry."
It's a wormy, ratty
little weasel – descended from a polecat.
Don't people kill it with sticks?
Eat it in stew?
I spelled it with a "u."
And to this day I have never been able
to eat
ferret.

Champion of 'em all receives prizes

Marianne Waters, fourteen-year-old eighth grader at the Donegal High School Annex, receives prizes from Harry F. Stacks, Intelligencer Journal editor, after she was named Grand Champion of the Intell Spelling Bee Friday night. Looking on are her parents, Chief Petty Officer and Mrs. Emory L. Waters, Florin, and her brothers and sister, Robert, twelve; Gary, nine, and Tena, eight.

Lancaster Intelligencer Journal Spelling Bee,
Lancaster, PA, 1963

the blessing of mount joy

two kinds of people live here
the ones who go to church and
the ones who go to the bar
had i stayed
i'd have become a raging alcoholic
or a hallelujah
or just climbed into my coffin
and slammed the lid -
these conservative folks
who didn't get me
or i them
they transformed me
into who i was intended to be
my mount joy family
a soul group family
who travels together over countless lifetimes
maybe next time around
i'll be the christian republican fundamentalist
and they'll be the renegades

The End is the Beginning – Muddying Your Own Holy Waters

I had to drink a lot of Tito's and smoke a lot of American Spirits (you know, that healthy brand) to get to the truths I've expressed in this collection. I'm revealing this not to shock you or to make you fear for my health. OK, maybe a little bit to shock you because I always enjoy doing that, but more importantly to explain how difficult it is for me to be vulnerable, to go beyond expressing my default reaction which is just to be majorly pissed off. And Lordess knows there's plenty in this world to be pissed off about and anger is a tremendously powerful sword. I'm not denigrating its muscle, but I don't want to live there. Ultimately, anger can be superficial and only go so far. It hasn't enabled me to get underneath my own masks. How much more there is to discover when the veil is penetrated – and so alcohol and cigarettes for me.

Writing these autobiographical poems has not been easy – or often much fun. It has, however, been exciting, challenging and much more difficult than I expected. In the long run it has been enlightening and freeing. Sometimes it has been hilariously funny and ironic. Who'd have thought that underneath my hurt and anger there lived love and compassion? Who'd have thought that a deeper understanding and forgiveness thrived there? For myself, for my family, for the people I love?

Your own process will be different, but I encourage you to explore it. Maybe you'll need to write under your favorite tree (if you're lucky enough to live in the country) or hang out at your local watering hole (if you're lucky enough to live in the city). Try not to smoke too many cigarettes.

Getting to the authentic bottom line of your life experiences will make you think and reflect. It will bring up emotions that were buried, seemingly lost in your everyday attempt just to survive on this crazy planet. The result, however, will surprise you – and more importantly it will liberate you. It will make you grateful for your own experiences, for all the hard times you went through. It will enable you to see those experiences in a new light and from a different point of view. It will make you love and appreciate the people and the family in your life that hurt and disappointed you but led you to become who you are.

Poetic expression is just one pathway to discover yourself, but it is a very powerful way. It doesn't matter if you consider yourself to be a poet. It just doesn't matter. There is no right or wrong way to express yourself poetically.

Here's a few exercises to start or continue your journey:

1. Write a poem about what would it look like to express something you've wanted to say but haven't been able to. Choose a family member or close friend. Don't hold back. Write as if no one will read it but you.

2. Create a poetic imagination about a person you'd like to forgive but haven't (can be yourself). What effect might forgiveness have on you or on the person you're forgiving? Are there benefits? Is there harm that can be healed?

3. Grieving is often associated with the death of a loved one, but there are many more aspects. Loss of possessions or opportunities or appearances or relationships etc. Write a poem about any loss in your life that you grieve.

Give it a try. I can help you explore other perspectives on your life's experiences, just by enabling you to feel safe enough to be honest with yourself. That friend who loved you so much she gave you nothing but support, those parents who experienced such trauma themselves that they couldn't see or appreciate you, that jerky teacher who yes, really was just a jerk.

I can point you in the direction of discovery, assist you in working through the darker places that are difficult to face. Each of us has these shadows, demons that are unique to our own experience, monsters we've harbored inside us that just mean we are human. Bringing them out of the darkness can free not only ourselves, but them.

Through the poetic process, I can coach you in finding the truth of your life's adventure. I can help make both the monsters and the friends encountered along the way, conscious, visible. I can support you in seeing them, valuing them. I can help you call an angel an angel or an asshole an asshole, but that's yours to decide.

Join my mailing list for weekly writing prompts. Let me coach you in your own authentic process. I'm always here to help you on your way – and I'm always on your side.

ChocPoet@gmail.com
www.chocolatewaters.com

CPSIA information can be obtained
at www.ICGtesting.com
Printed in the USA
BVHW051600131021
618743BV00018B/115